Little Math Stories

Sort the Beads

By Amanda Gebhardt

2 Wen will sort these beads.

How many are there?

4 How many red?

How many blue?

6 Wen can sort red beads here.

Wen can sort blue beads here.

Wen can slip one red
bead on this string.

Then Wen can add
one blue bead.

Wen can add more red beads.

Wen can add more blue beads.

Wen made a pattern.

Wen ties the string.
It is a gift for Fern.

Word List

math words

add	more
How	pattern
many	sort

sight words

a	one
How	the
many	

r-controlled vowels

/ar/ are	/er/ er	/ear/ ere	/air/ ere	/or/ or, ore
are	Fern	here	there	for
	pattern			more
				sort

Try It!

Sort beads or colored paper into piles by color. Use the piles to make a pattern. What can you make?

14

69 Words

Wen will sort these beads.

How many are there?

How many red?

How many blue?

Wen can sort red beads here.

Wen can sort blue beads here.

Wen can slip one red bead on this string.

Then Wen can add one blue bead.

Wen can add more red beads. Wen can add
more blue beads. Wen made a pattern.

Wen ties the string. It is a gift for Fern.

CHERRY BLOSSOM PRESS

Published in the United States of America by Cherry Lake Publishing Group
Ann Arbor, Michigan
www.cherrylakepublishing.com

Photo Credits: Cover: © Wirestock Creators/Shutterstock.com; pages 3-5, 10-13: © Cherry Lake Publishing; pages 6-7: © Lane Erickson/Dreamstime.com; pages 8-9: © Fizkes/Dreamstime.com; page 15, Back Cover: © pattara puttiwong/Shutterstock.com

Cherry Blossom Press is an imprint of Cherry Lake Publishing Group.

Library of Congress Cataloging-in-Publication Data has been filed and is available at catalog.loc.gov.

Cherry Lake Publishing Group would like to acknowledge the work of the Partnership for 21st Century Learning, a Network of Battelle for Kids. Please visit http://www.battelleforkids.org/networks/p21 for more information.

Printed in the United States of America
Corporate Graphics

Amanda Gebhardt is a curriculum writer and editor and a life-long learner. She lives in Ann Arbor, Michigan, with her husband, two kids, and one playful pup named Cookie.